MW00655075

Don't pick a fight with the Giles girls!

— Andrew Breitbart

Regis' niche is as the ambassadress of the polished trigger finger.

— Nina Burleigh, ELLE Magazine

At weekends she is one of the deadliest shots in the brush.

— Jeff Maysh, Daily Mail

Dedication

This book is dedicated to my parents who raised me to be the strong, independent woman I am today and my jujutsu instructors Pedro Valente, Gui Valente, Joaquim Valente, James Robertson, Burak Eyilik and Joel Infante who trained me to be fully equipped to defend such an existence. Your wisdom and guidance has helped form me into the person I am today. Thank you.

HOW TO NOT BE A #METOO VICTIM, BUT A #WARRIORCHICK

WRITTEN BY

REGIS GILES

ISBN 978-1-61808-167-4

Printed in the United States of America

Cover design created by Ron Bell of AdVision Design Group (www.advisiondesigngroup.com)

Cover photos courtesy of Michael Fell
www.mikefellphotography.com
Instagram - @mikefellsafaris

Disclaimer

The author of this book is not an attorney, nor is she licensed to practice law in any state. Laws about firearms and the use of deadly force vary from jurisdiction to jurisdiction and are continually changing. Take the time and effort to research your jurisdiction as the law may be more or less strict where you live. Again - consult the best attorney you can afford.

Table of Contents

Acknowledgments

I would like to acknowledge my father Doug Giles who motivated me to write this book, my publishers Skip and Sara Coryell for believing in this book, my editors Steve Pauwels and Connie Hill-Coryell, photographer Michael Fell for taking the cover photos, and all of my loved ones who advised and encouraged me while writing this book. Your time has been greatly appreciated. Thank you.

Introduction

The Harvey Weinstein sexual misconduct allegations have sparked a flame in an already fuel-doused forest of angry, wounded women and men across the globe. While the month of October 2017 proved woeful for Weinstein and his monstrous behavior, it has been equally sucky for others who have committed similar offenses. Yes, the sexual predators who've victimized many an unsuspecting soul in the work environment – be it an encounter in the office or a business meeting outside are no longer able to creep along and hide in the dark with their threats.

Today is a new day for those who were targeted and are victims of sexual abuse. Actresses, journalists, producers and assistants have come forward, voicing the wrongs that have been done against them by said predators. It is inspiring to see women and men alike finally feeling brave enough to publicly speak about such traumatic events.

No one, unless they've been in the same situation, can ever really understand the stress and self-doubt one goes through when something like this occurs. Do I want this to be happening? Why is his hand on my waist? Is he really fondling my breasts? What do I do? Why is he in a bathrobe? Why is he taking off the bathrobe? God, I need to get out of here. I thought this was going to be professional.

After the encounter comes the self-doubt and bullying. The man whom you denied calls you a c**t, proclaiming that your career is over. So you shut up about what happened, bury it deep inside and live life in fear.

These scenarios are understandable. A lot of people, naive to the monsters that lurk in the "Big Offices," can easily walk into such problems.

Now that we have a global spotlight on sexual predators, we equally need to shine a light on how to beat the living poop out of any predator who might try to harm you. That is where I come in.

— Regis Giles

Chapter 1

The Sexual Abuse

Epidemic

"Life, liberty, and property do not exist because men have made laws. On the contrary, it was the fact that life, liberty, and property existed beforehand that caused men to make laws in the first place."

— Frédéric Bastiat, The Law

The Sexual Abuse Epidemic

I F YOU CAN BELIEVE ANY STATISTICS published by our government (fingers crossed they got this one right) the numbers published on rape and sexual assault between the years 2014-15 are staggering.

The U.S. Justice Department's Bureau of Justice Statistics published in their study on Criminal Victimization, 2015, that there were a reported 284,350 rapes/sexual assaults in 2014. In 2015, that number jumped to 431,840. Quite a significant bounce. Go ahead and peruse the table on the next page.

Violent victimization, by type of violent crime, 2014 and 2015

Type of violent crime	Number		Rate per 1,000 persons age 12 or older	
	2014*	2015	2014*	2015
Violent crime[a]	5,359,570	5,006,620	20.1	18.6
Rape/sexual assault[b]	284,350	431,840†	1.1	1.6†
Robbery	664,210	578,580	2.5	2.1
Assault	4,411,010	3,996,200	16.5	14.8
Aggravated assault	1,092,090	816,760‡	4.1	3.0‡
Simple assault	3,318,920	3,179,440	12.4	11.8
Domestic violence[c]	1,109,880	1,094,660	4.2	4.1
Intimate partner violence[d]	634,610	806,050‡	2.4	3.0
Stranger violence	2,166,130	1,821,310	8.1	6.8
Violent crime involving injury	1,375,950	1,303,290	5.2	4.8
Serious violent crime[e]	2,040,650	1,827,170	7.7	6.8
Serious domestic violence[c]	400,030	460,450	1.5	1.7
Serious intimate partner violence[d]	265,890	333,210	1.0	1.2
Serious stranger violence	930,690	690,550‡	3.5	2.6
Serious violent crime involving weapons	1,306,960	977,840†	4.9	3.6†
Serious violent crime involving injury	692,470	658,040	2.6	2.4

Note: Detail may not sum to total due to rounding. Total population age 12 or older was 266,665,160 in 2014 and 269,526,470 in 2015. See appendix table 2 for standard errors.
*Comparison year.
†Significant difference from comparison year at 95% confidence level.
‡Significant difference from comparison year at 90% confidence level.
[a]Excludes homicide because the NCVS is based on interviews with victims and therefore cannot measure murder.
[b]BJS has initiated projects examining collection methods for self-report data on rape and sexual assault. See *NCVS measurement of rape and sexual assault in Methodology* for more information.
[c]Includes victimization committed by intimate partners and family members.
[d]Includes victimization committed by current or former spouses, boyfriends, or girlfriends.
[e]In the NCVS, serious violent crime includes rape or sexual assault, robbery, and aggravated assault.
Source: Bureau of Justice Statistics, National Crime Victimization Survey (NCVS), 2014 and 2015.

The Bureau of Justice Statistics defines these two crimes as:

Rape - Forced sexual intercourse including both psychological coercion as well as physical force. Forced sexual intercourse means penetration by the offender(s). Includes attempted rapes, male as well as female victims, and both heterosexual and same sex rape.

Attempted rape includes verbal threats of rape.

Sexual assault - A wide range of victimizations, separate from rape or attempted rape. These crimes include attacks or attempted attacks generally involving unwanted sexual contact between victim and offender. Sexual assaults may or may not involve force and include such things as grabbing or fondling. It also includes verbal threats.

> 284,350 rapes/ sexual assaults in 2014
> It rose to 431,840 in 2015.

Now, I could continue to bombard you with multiple statistics showing how rape and sexual abuse is still a prevalent crime, but it won't get to the heart of the matter.

What matters is you.

Your life, and your natural right to protect your life. End of story.

So, what is the phenomenon? Why are so many women and men being subjected to these crimes?

The old-school thinking of just sit there and take it so you don't get hurt any further has been replaced with today's feminist mantra "teach men not to rape."

Both methods are equally stupid.

Why? First, clearly neither approach has worked. Secondly, it defies logic.

> Today's feminist mantra is "Teach men not to rape."

Sexual abuse and rape are acts of violence against your person. Would you say it is logical at that point in time to defend your life?

YYYYEEEEESSSSSSSS!!!

And anyone who says, "no" should have their brain checked, stat. They could be mentally unbalanced or the next Jeffrey Dahmer.

Seriously, get them examined.

It is a natural right, given to everyone upon existence, to be able to defend and protect your life, freedom and property.

There is nothing wrong with fighting back! It is your instinct and, I would debate, your moral obligation.

And EVERYONE'S first line of defense should always be to not put yourself in dangerous situations.

For example:

- walking down dark alleys
- getting ridiculously intoxicated
- traveling alone to certain areas…again, the alley; JUST DON'T DO IT!
- leaving your blinds open in your home at night
- parking in bad areas

These instances open up the door to all sorts of dangerous encounters.

The concept of self-defense isn't new and frankly came well before the 9th Century, when the Chinese first invented gunpowder.

> You are legally and morally obligated to fight back!

Where is the proof, you say?

Glad you asked.

Let's look at the great Exodus of the Hebrews from

Egyptian enslavement.

Upon establishing themselves as a free people, one of their rules became, interestingly enough: If a thief is caught breaking in at night, you're supposed to cower in a corner, beg them to leave and scream for help. Oh no, wait; that's not what it says.

What it does say is,

> "If a thief is caught breaking in at night and is struck a fatal blow, the defender is not guilty of bloodshed".

Exodus 22:2

Put another way: It's self-defense, not murder. Sounds a lot like today's castle doctrine, does it not?

So here you have an ancient civilization, free from tyranny and enslavement, establishing laws to maintain that freedom, and they all understood defending your life was right, a necessary right.

Even the Bible teaches us that self-defense is a moral act.

Let's fast forward a couple of centuries now to the great political philosopher and lawyer Cicero.

This man believed in self-defense so much that he had major issues with people who waited for help rather than acting on instinct.

Check out his quote:

> "For people who DECIDE to wait for
> these will have to wait for justice,
> too—and meanwhile they must suffer
> injustice first."

— Cicero

Cicero understood what many of our politicians today don't understand.

In the face of adversity, especially to your own life, you have to act or suffer injustice first.

… and that suffering is a big gamble, one that risks your life.

Whether you choose to flee the situation or stand and fight, it is yours to assess and address.

Essentially, Cicero would not advise you to call 911 when an attacker is charging at you full-steam-ahead, ready to kill.

> You can escape
> or you can
> stand your
> ground, but the
> choice is yours.

He would, however, tell you it is your right to stand and fight using force because it's common sense!

The quote continues:

> "Indeed, even the wisdom of a law

itself, by sort of tacit implication, permits self-defense, because it is not actually forbidden to kill; what it does, instead, is to forbid the bearing of a weapon with the intention to kill."

Ancient civilization and one of the most influential Roman philosophers understood self-defense as perfectly logical.

If you still are on the fence as to whether there is a right to defend your life, look at some of your body's natural reflexes.

> Self-defense is your body's natural reaction to danger.

- If someone snaps their fingers in your eyes, do you blink?

- When someone pinches you, do you stay there and take it, or jerk your body away from the pain?

- If someone decides to choke you, are you just going to let them? No, your instinct is to escape the pain, by whatever means necessary.

Self-preservation is natural and often times that comes in different methods.

Chapter 2

Kick Ass Using

Any Method

"There exists a law, not written down anywhere, but inborn in our hearts; a law which comes to us not by training or custom or reading but by derivation and absorption and adoption from nature itself; a law which has come to us not from theory but from practice, not by instruction but by natural intuition. I refer to the law which lays it down that, if our lives are endangered by plots or violence or armed robbers or enemies, any and every method of protecting ourselves is morally right. When weapons reduce them to silence, the laws no longer expect one to wait their pronouncements. For people who decide to wait for these will have to wait for justice, too—and meanwhile they must suffer injustice first. Indeed, even the wisdom of a law itself, by sort of tacit implication, permits self-defense, because it is not actually forbidden to kill; what it does, instead, is to forbid the bearing of a weapon with the intention to kill. When, therefore, inquiry passes beyond the mere question of the weapon and starts to consider the motive, a man who has used arms in self-defense is not regarded as having carried with a homicidal aim." – Marcus Tullius Cicero, "In Defence of Titus Annus Milo," in Selected Speeches of Cicero (Michael Grant translator and editor, 1969.)

Kick Ass Using
Any Method

I HAVE BEEN A JUJUTSU STUDENT AT the Valente Brothers Academy since the age of nine and I love it! I highly recommend this comprehensive fighting system. It's second to none.

I also train with firearms for self-defense and have fiddled with the occasional knife, Taser, and tomahawk. You should certainly consider thoroughly training with guns. They provide minimal effort and maximum results.

In the moment of an attack, would it not be logical to use any method I saw fit to protect myself?

Yes.

Some feminists don't believe that, and a perpetrator

might even sue you for hurting them while they were trying to sexually abuse or rape you. However, that does not prove it is illogical for you to use the method of defense of your choice.

So, do you have the right to defend your life in any way you choose?

Before we dive into that question, let me share a personal story with you.

> Throughout history self-defense has been a natural and logical choice.

Back in middle school, an acquaintance of mine was raped. For the sake of her privacy I'm going to call her Helen.

The event took place at a North Miami, Florida middle school. A sidewalk with heavy shrubs and forestry on one side of it lined a path to get back and forth from the school to a parent vehicle pick-up point.

It was a commonly traveled path by students, but was further from the school and "out of the way" of heavy human traffic areas.

Helen skipped class one day and, while walking down this path, away from school grounds, two guys attacked her and raped her.

Why they were there and how they knew she would be there, I don't know.

What happened to her was TERRIBLE and very unfortunate. It hit all of us in school hard, but Helen's life was never the same after that. Seeing the psychological difficulties she went through after the attack and how she as a person completely changed was scary to witness.

> If you are a victim of rape, your life will never be the same.

As much as I loathe what happened to Helen, the situation could have been completely avoided. I don't say this to be cold or heartless; quite the contrary. If Helen had been in class, where she should have been, this rape would never have occurred.

Helen placed herself in harm's way.

Now certain individuals would suggest that the answer to this problem would be to teach those attackers not to rape. In general, I think most parents are not teaching their children rape is a good thing to do.

But part of owning your life means that you don't put yourself in harm's way. That's instinct, right? Remember the blinking eyes?

Helen's instinct was inhibited at the time of her attack, so her situational awareness wasn't at the level it should have been.

I am NOT saying that the rape was her fault, all I am

saying is that it could have been avoided easily.

Let's switch the scenario here to something hypo-thetical.

Helen is a senior in college. She is walking to a night class from the campus parking lot when she is at-tacked suddenly from behind. Several blows are made to her face. Conscious, she is dragged to a side alley and, with a knife to her throat, is about to get raped.

> You are morally justified in using deadly force to prevent rape.

At this moment, should Helen be able to use any meth-od of defense to get away from this attacker?

Absolutely!

Furthermore, it is morally right for her to use any and every method, because her intentions are to defend herself; to stop someone from violating her life, liberty and property.

If she chose to use a stick, brick, shard of glass, knife, Taser, jujutsu or a gun, all would be logical means of protection.

Suppose Helen was one of those people who used a gun to defend her life.

In our society today on a yearly basis, many people have used a firearm to defend themselves —close to

2.5 million.

But some individuals believe that, due to a possibility that Helen's gun might be taken away from her and used against her, she shouldn't use a firearm.

The CATO Institute did a study on the use of firearms in self-defense and their findings on this specific scenario were interesting.

During a time frame between October 2003 through November 2011, 227 incidents were reported where the intended victim DISARMED the attacker, while eleven attackers disarmed the victim.

The numbers would suggest then that the risk is minimal and Helen was logical for using a gun to defend her life. Banning a gun for the possibility of it being used in a harmful manner is the same thinking as outlawing swimming pools for the possibility of a person drowning.

More good comes from a person being armed than comes from a person being disarmed because it takes less courage for an assailant to attack an unarmed person than it does for them to attack an armed person.

> Every year 2.5 million people use a firearm to defend themselves.

That's why you see spikes in violent crime in Chicago, which is our nation's most gun-controlled city. It's a criminal's paradise, a pond of sitting ducks.

Lucky for Helen, she lived in a state where she was able to keep herself armed.

Just imagine what would have happened to her if she didn't.

Whatever method you choose to defend your life, know how to do it well.

From what I have learned with my seventeen years of training in jujutsu, you don't have time to think in the heat of the moment, only to react. You can take up to thirty-six classes of hand-to-hand self-defense and have enough reflex to respond to a life-threatening situation.

> Most altercations are extremely sudden and very violent.

Train your body to have those reflexes so that you have the best possible chance of survival. In life, nothing is a guarantee, but what we can do is prepare ourselves for the worst. As Archilochus, a Greek soldier from 650 BC, said, "We do not rise to the level of our expectations. We fall to the level of our training."

I'm not saying because you practice a method of defense you won't ever get attacked or potentially killed, but the odds are more in your favor if you do and fewer people will mess with you. They will be able to see the confidence in you simply by the way you walk.

I wish we lived in a world where we didn't have to do this; where everyone lived in harmony and the respect for our fellow human was understood and never violated; where gang violence, terrorism and even suicide didn't exist.

But the line that divides good and evil goes right through the heart of every individual. This insightful statement was made by a man who certainly knew what evil was: the Russian novelist and Nobel Prize winner Aleksandr Solzhenitsyn, who was an outspoken critic of the Soviet Union & communism, and raised global awareness of its Gulag forced labor camp system.

> Your confidence level, though subjective, will be noticed and help to deter an attacker.

So, is self-defense logical? Yes. Is the use of any method to protect your life logical? Yes.

BUT...

The key to a safe society is not through the regulation of guns, Tasers, pepper-spray, knives, billy clubs, or any other weapon, but rather through the regulation of the heart, something achieved only by the combined influence of morality and education.

Once we start focusing on the heart of society and less on banning certain types of weapons, then we will start seeing real results.

Helpful Resources

Valente Brothers Academy

To learn more about the Valente Brothers
Academy, go to www.graciemiami.com.
com or call them at (305) 354 2060.

They are located at:
16360 26th Avenue,
North Miami Beach, FL 33160

Chapter 3

Get Street Smart, Ladies!

"Civilized people are taught by logic, barbarians by necessity, communities by tradition; and lesson is inculcated even in wild beasts by nature itself. They learn that they have to defend their own bodies and persons and lives from violence of any and every kind by all the means within their power."

— Marcus Tullius Cicero, "In Defence of Titus Annus Milo," in Selected Speeches of Cicero (Michael Grant translator and editor, 1969.)

Get Street Smart, Ladies!

U NTIL SOCIETY DECIDES TO FIX the real heart of the problem, there is an immediate issue that must be addressed: The act of sexual assault and/or rape.

Feminists' solution to this is teaching men not to rape. Generally, most people know rape is an evil thing to do; even the person committing the act knows.

So how does one go about "correcting" this problem?

Well, an armed society is a polite society. Women and men learning how to fight and defend their lives is the best way to reduce a criminal problem. Quite literally, by you protecting your own life, you teach the thugs of this world "manners."

To wit, you and your loved ones are not to be

messed with because there will be serious consequences. However, before you run off to a self-defense academy or go buy a gun, there are precautions you can use right now that are hardwired in your body.

> Your gut instincts are like an early-warning system. Always listen to them.

While reading the below precautions, I encourage you to highlight and check off the security defenses you already have hardwired into your reflexes.

Personal Defense:

First off, listen to your gut. Sometimes our bodies give us a warning that something is not right. Humans often ignore this feeling.

For example, when a big time Hollywood producer & movie mogul invites you up to his hotel room to discuss "business" and he answers the door in his bathrobe, you don't go inside. This is the moment your gut should be screaming at you, "This is not right!"

The gut knows best.

It is our sixth sense, a divine gift that can easily be ignored if our senses are inhibited.

So, here is the second tip: don't volunteer to be vulnerable. The best way to avoid a problem is by not putting yourself in a problematic position.

Let's say you're out partying with your friends and you decide to get wasted (bad choice number one). Should you choose to drink, getting wasted greatly inhibits your senses and your ability to react to a life-threatening situation.

In this state, you might even unintentionally place yourself in such a scenario.

Imagine, stumbling drunk to your Uber and you can't locate the pickup point for your hired drive. You accidentally walk down a side path that leads you to a dark road. None of your friends are around and it's just you.

> You will live or die based on decisions you make, so always make good choices.

This scenario is bad enough for a person who is armed and sober, let alone someone who is drunk and solo.

The best way to avoid getting stuck in a vulnerable position is being aware of where you are, who you're with and what you're capable of.

Know the environment you are in. If you know the landscape, a quick entrance and exit is possible, as well as determining if the area is safe for you to travel and what the assumed risks could be if any should occur.

Be aware of the people surrounding you and, yes,

judge them. You need to be able to assess if a person is a threat or not. Look at their mannerisms and study their behavior. If your gut tells you something is seriously off, get out of there and notify officials.

Should you come face-to-face with a suspicious person, I give you permission to be rude if you have to. There's no reason to be nice to creeps. Speak assertively and with confidence.

> It's okay to be rude when you feel you are in danger.

Knowing what you are capable of will also determine how you respond to certain situations. Let's say the office pervert tries to corner you in the recreational room while you're grabbing a cup of coffee. You can:

1. Yell at him for being a creep.

2. Shuffle to the side of him and walk away, giving him no recognition that he exists.

3. Should he try to get physical, toss the coffee in his face and knee him in the groin.

Every scenario is viable, depending on the threat level; and your gut will tell you what answer is necessary.

(GET VOCAL SO PEOPLE KNOW YOU'RE THE ONE GETTING ATTACKED.)

Also be aware of how you react under stress. With this knowledge you will be able to determine the right kind of training you need to improve on or sharpen, to make your ability that much greater in a stressful situation.

The most important thing to do is to have a plan for your personal safety.

If you're going on a date with someone you barely know, meet them at the place instead of having them pick you up. When on the date, be upfront about your interests and limitations; and know that sexual assaults and rape can happen anywhere, anytime and to anyone. Also, tell your family or friends where you are going and give them the person's contact information, should you go missing and authorities need to track him/her down.

> Always have an escape plan for any imaginable self-defense scenario.

If you're wanting to further advance your career and some big time hot-shot says he can help you, don't meet him in private.

Hello!

It sends all the wrong signals about yourself and to him. Keep all professional business in public places and, if possible, have a third party present.

Don't allow anyone to shame you into anything you do not want to do. Know exactly what you will and will not accept. Have standards!

Be firm with your "NOs" and take no prisoners should anyone violate your standards.

Home Defense:

> Situational awareness is key to avoiding danger. Always stay alert.

When it comes to your home, never let your guard down. Though it is your safe haven, being situationally aware in this environment is critical to maintain that feeling of safety and comfort.

So, when a stranger knocks on your door, don't answer. If you're not expecting anyone and you can see from a secure vantage, by an undetectable glance through the window or through security cameras, that you don't know the person, like I said earlier, permission to be rude. If you hear a strange noise outside, don't go outside! Should it really concern you, call the police.

If there is an instance of compassion for a stranded motorist asking to use your phone, let them wait outside. The point is, don't let any stranger into your home.

Should you have repairmen coming to your home,

be sure you're properly clothed and that other people are with you. Also, verify the worker's identification before he comes inside.

If you're home alone, don't tell a stranger this. In this moment, it is important that you have the proper security for your home: The doors have the safest locks on them, your windows are secure and your spare key isn't outside, waiting to be found by an intruder.

> Never let anyone shame you into letting them into your home.

Should there be areas of your home or apartment that lack the proper security measures, for example, bad lighting or a broken window, get them fixed ASAP. There is no sense in having all this security if there is a weak point.

Make your bedroom a fortress of safety. Once again, put the best locks on your bedroom door and make sure the windows are secure. Have a phone in the room should an intruder come in. If you've been trained with weapons, keep one near.

If you're gone from your home, leave a few lights on. This will usually keep thieves away. Also, keep your blinds or curtains closed at night to avoid giving anyone with bad-intentions the ability to case your place. Make sure they are closed properly so others can't see in from the outside.

Finally, know your neighbors. They could be of great help to you in a time of need.

Women Protecting Their "Castle":

In 2017, there were multiple instances of home invasions reported in which women protected their castles from dangerous people:

> A woman's home is her castle. Harden your home against crime.

Kay Dickinson was attacked on January 2, 2017, while entering her apartment in Wilmington, North Carolina, after getting off of work. News station WWAY reported, "The suspect held her at gunpoint, beat her and then tied her up with a broken belt in her bedroom." Able to escape her bondages, she grabbed her gun and killed the intruder.

Kim Badger of Charlotte, North Carolina, had her home invaded by a suspect armed with a baseball bat on January 20, 2017. According to WCNC, the attacker hit Badger with the bat, then chased her throughout the house. Badger put up a fight, denying the attacker the ability to take control of a knife on the counter and even access to a sword. Her son entered into the mix, which gave Badger the opportunity to get her gun and shoot the suspect dead.

A man brought his seven-year-old son along for a home invasion on May 12, 2017, attempting to break into the house through a window. The female home-owner happened to be sleeping in the same room. Upon hearing the suspect, she armed herself and fired two rounds. The San Antonio Express-News reported that the man was transported to a hospital after police arrived, where he was later pronounced dead.

Fox 59 reports a mother protecting her children opened fire and killed a home invader who was trying to break in during the daytime on June 7, 2017. She came face-to-face with the suspect, Michael Hawkins, and opened fire in that moment. He dropped dead in the doorway. Luckily, the mother and her children were unharmed.

Kimber Wood, 17, called her dad after being alerted of a car thief near her family's home, and asked if she could get one of his guns, just in case any-thing happened. She was right to ask, because the thief broke into her home. The criminal fled her house after she ordered him to go and he saw the gun. Kimber took chase to the suspect and fired a warning shot, showing she wasn't afraid to use the weapon. This happened on July 17, 2017.

> If you are attacked, you must fight hard and never give up!

On July 31, 2017, two home invaders broke into the wrong grandma's house. According to ABC 13, a 60 yr.-old grandmother was in her house alone, when the criminals broke in through her garage. Harris County Deputy Thomas Gilliland said, "Both were armed with pistols. She confronted both suspects, retrieved a handgun and fired several times at both subjects." One was killed in the exchange.

These women had the training and mindset ready to prevent any life-threatening scenario in their homes, and look at the results. They won and the bad guys didn't, and that is beautiful.

> To prevail in an armed confrontation, you'll need proper training.

Out and About Defense:

Now, when it comes to your personal security when working out outside or just walking around, you might want to consider the following pointers:

Don't do it alone. A crowd is harder to beat up or target than a person flying solo.

Be aware of your surroundings and if anyone is following you, either in a car or on foot. If they are following you, create distance from them and try to lose them. It is easy to turn the opposite direction and run away, but stay in public and notify the authorities. You really need to trust your gut in situations like this.

When walking around, don't look lost. Keep your

posture and know where you are going; if you don't...
pretend like you do.

Wear clothes that you can maneuver in should the
need to run or fight arise.

If you're working out outside, keep your headsets
off and don't stare down at your phone. These are dis-
tractions from your immediate surroundings and dull
your senses.

If you're walking home late
from partying or down any
sidewalk at any time of day,
take the middle path. Don't be
too close to cars or shrubbery
where someone can pop out and
grab you.

> **If you look
> like a sheep,
> you'll be eaten
> by wolves.**

Keep your distance from vehicles that pull over to
ask you a question. If you can't hear them, tell the person to speak up or just walk away. You don't owe them
anything.

Also, whenever outside, face the flow of car traffic.
Doing so will prevent any surprise attack from behind.

Know the area you're traveling to on foot. Figure
out what areas are safe to go to and what ones are not.
Think ahead: "If I were in serious trouble, I would run
to [insert name of store or safe place here]."

Should you have any physical impediments, plan

ahead for ease in accessing certain places.

Be suspicious of everyone. Never let your guard down.

Workplace Defense:

> Be extra alert in transitional spaces like parking lots.

If there is someone at work whom you believe is a threat to your personal safety, notify Human Resources and your boss; don't find yourself stuck in a room with that person and avoid them at all costs. Don't be timid or fearful around them, however. Show boldness and that you won't be intimidated.

Know the blueprints of the office. Is there more than one exit? Stairwells, elevators? What escape routes can you take?

Make sure all safety measures are taken into account in your workplace. If you see there is something lacking, suggest some changes to your boss.

If there is any guest in the office who seems suspicious, ask for their identification and ask why they are there. Trust your gut at this point; if something is off you might be right.

Should you find yourself working in the office alone, keep the doors locked and avoid letting strangers in. And if you're working late, see if a co-worker will stay with you so that you're not walking out alone.

Approaching Your Car Defense:

Clearly, keeping your car locked is the best way to prevent any unwanted entry. Always lock it – even if you're at the gas pump filling up your car.

If you're sitting in the car, the doors are locked, too. You don't want any unwanted people stepping in.

When approaching your car, have the keys ready so you can get into your car with no problem.

> Analyze your workplace and have a plan to escape or defend.

Also, check your car before entering. If there is anything suspicious about your vehicle, walk away and call the authorities if you need to. The last thing you want is someone to attack you from the backseat of your own car while driving.

Should someone be under your car and grab your ankle, stomp the crap out of their hands with your free leg. Also, pulling up hard with your captured foot should release the grip.

Let's say an attacker attempts to force his way into your car. The best thing you can do is to grab your keys and/or get out! Let them take the car if that's what they want. That is much better than you getting kidnapped and potentially killed.

Traveling with Your Car Defense:

Always keep the tank full. You don't want to be on empty in a bad neighborhood or some Texas Chainsaw Massacre place.

Should your vehicle break down, know your location and make your car your fortress: Windows and doors locked. Wait for help from AAA or a company equivalent to it. If a pedestrian stops, don't get out of the car and either have them call for help or tell them you've got help on the way.

Carry a road flare with you to signal car mechanical problems. You can also raise the hood of your car. Once this is done, get back to your fortress.

> Always check the back seat before getting into your car.

Be sure to have enough money and make sure your cell phone is charged should car emergencies occur and you need to hire a car.

If an aggressive driver bumps you from behind and you're not comfortable getting out of your car, drive to a police station and don't get out of the vehicle until it is safe.

Should you suspect someone is following you, don't lead them to your home or place of business.

Once again, drive to the police station or fire station and get their attention. Don't get out of the vehicle until it is safe.

Also, don't pick up hitchhikers or help stranded motorists. If you want to help, call authorities and tell them the location.

Busses, Trains and Elevators Defense:

If you're using public transportation, when waiting at the station stand in a strategic position, so you can't get pulled into a car; have a barrier between you and the road.

> Don't get involved in road rage. Try to disengage and call nine-one-one.

Sit close to a group of people, instead of secluded, especially at night time when the bus and trains are practically empty. If possible, sit close to the driver and near an exit, preferably in an aisle seat. Don't find yourself stuck in a seat because someone is blocking you in. Always think of quick escapes.

Get up and move from your seat should you ever feel uncomfortable; and don't fall asleep. Stay alert at all times and don't let your smartphones or headsets distract you.

Be alert for suspicious people or packages. Terrorist

attacks have occurred too many times on public transport routes. Should you run across something, alert the driver and notify police.

When hiring a ride, be sure to verify that person's identification before entering the vehicle.

Elevators are a confined space. Be sure to check what is in the elevator before getting on. Avoid groups of men if that makes you uncomfortable and get the next lift.

Stand near the control panel of the elevator, so you have quick access to ring the alarm if you have to; and make sure you're near the doors so you can escape quickly if need be. You can also push as many elevator buttons as possible to have an opportunity to get off on the next floor.

> There is safety in numbers. Always travel with a friend when you can.

Hotel Defense:

When checking into a hotel, make sure the people at the front desk keep your private information private. Ask them to please write it down if they need you to verify anything in their records. You don't want some creep hearing all your personal contact information.

Don't give out your room number to strange people; only to someone you trust and have known for a while.

When entering your room, check its security. Make sure all the locks on the doors and windows work. Also, use a bug sweeper in your room to find any hidden video cameras or audio recorders.

Should strangers knock on your door, don't open it; and if they persist tell them to leave and call the police if you need to. Notify the hotel, also.

In the wake of the mass shooting at the Las Vegas Strip in Nevada during the Route 91 Harvest music festival, one should be extra alert to suspicious people and noises. Stephen Paddock shot from the Mandalay Bay hotel on the 32nd floor, killing 58 people and injuring 546.

These are all methods that can be implemented in your daily routine starting now. What I would like you to do is take a few moments and write down in the blank pages below areas in which you could improve. Also, jot down any items you might need to purchase to ensure your defense is at its highest level.

> Keep your hotel room locked, and don't let in strangers.

Personal Notes

_____

_____

_____

_____

_____

_____

_____

_____

_____

_____

_____

_____

_____

_____

_____

_____

_____

Personal Notes

_____

_____

_____

_____

_____

_____

_____

_____

_____

_____

_____

_____

_____

_____

_____

_____

_____

Personal Notes

Chapter 4

Be Ready for a Fight —

Get the Boldness Inside

You to Say "NO!"

"Love toward oneself remains a fundamental principle of morality. Therefore, it is legitimate to insist on respect for one's own right to life. Someone who defends his life is not guilty of murder even if he is forced to deal his aggressor a lethal blow: 'If a man in self-defense uses more than necessary violence, it will be unlawful: whereas if he repels force with moderation, his defense will be lawful ... Nor is it necessary for salvation that a man omit the act of moderate self-defense to avoid killing the other man, since one is bound to take more care of one's own life than of another's.'

"Legitimate defense can be not only a right but a grave duty for one who is responsible for the lives of others. The defense of the common good requires that an unjust aggressor be rendered unable to cause harm."

Catechism of the Catholic Church, paragraphs 2263-65 (1997). Internal quotations are from Thomas Aquinas, Summa Theologica, Second Part of the Second Part, Question 64, Article 7

Be Ready for a Fight — Get the Boldness Inside You to Say "NO!"

SHOULD SOMEONE VIOLATE YOUR standards and ignore your warnings, this is the moment you must decide: fight or flight?

If you have the ability to run away from such situations, a good run is better than a bad stand.

However, if you are stuck and have to fight for your life, then be sure you know how to do so because, guess what? That person attacking you has no regard for your well-being and will probably respond with greater resistance once you decide to fight back.

This does not mean you should be afraid of the fight; it means you need to be prepared for any hits that might come your way and understand you are not looking to win the fight, you are looking to survive.

What does that mean?

Often, when someone is training in self-defense in any form, they imagine themselves the victor by choking the person out, breaking a limb or two, or hitting them with a knock-out blow. What we imagine and what is reality are two different things.

> Be prepared to fight, but avoid it whenever possible.

Your goal in an instance of personal attack should be to stop the attack prior to the assault if possible and/or address the violence with the appropriate techniques. Going into a physical altercation with the idea that you are going to win is the wrong mindset and could set you up for failure.

SURVIVE!

Forcing the "win" will exhaust you and lead you to many mistakes, including ticking off your attacker.

Address the assault with the appropriate self-defense techniques, waiting for your opportunity to then get your attacker in a choke hold or some other submissive move after they make a mistake.

Most importantly, keep your mind clear and emotionless. This will allow you to respond to any sexual assault or rape attempt in the most effective and efficient way possible.

Should you choose to get emotional, your decision making process becomes clouded and a sense of panic overcomes you, often causing a "freeze" sensation.

If you are trained with the ability to respond to any offense, you should be clear minded and capable of avoiding that "freeze" moment. You don't need seventeen years of training to attain this either.

Just because you train in self-defense doesn't mean you won't encounter such situations or that you won't potentially "freeze" if you do. Rely on your ability to react to a threat! Let the reflexes of your training do the job.

When you decide to fight and you use deadly force in self-defense, the legal system will hold it up to the standard of "the reasonable person". This sort of scale is based on questions like: "Would any reasonable thinking person do what you did, under the same circumstances, knowing exactly what you knew in that moment? Would they have used deadly force?"

> In times of high stress, your emotions can cloud your decision-making process.

Often times it is better to be judged by twelve, than carried by six; however, knowing the kind of legal battle you face could help in your decision making on what sort of reasonable force you will use in self-defense situations.

Regis Giles with her first kudu, a nice old bull. Using her 9.3x62 CZ 550 rifle.

Regis Giles looking through the scope of an AR-15.

Regis and her father Doug Giles in Alaska.

Here Regis is shooting for the first time a
full-auto rifle.

Regis with her Texas Dall Sheep. Shot using her
.30/30 Winchester built in 1941, using open sights.

Regis in her dad's office with dogs Ruger and Danger sporting a 1895 Winchester chambered in US .30 Gov't. (Photo: Ben Philippi)

Hunting wild boar in Florida's wilderness with her 9.3X62 rifle. Regis enjoys hunting without the use scopes if possible.

Regis tags along during a friend's hunt in Del Rio, TX., armed with her favorite .30/30 Winchester and a camera.

Regis with her sister Hannah (left) who is also a
Valente Brothers black belt.

Learn about all things Regis Giles at her website

www.girlsjustwannahaveguns.com

Chapter 5

Legal Use of Force

"It is not good for us that we should lose the fighting quality. We shall have lost something vital and beyond price on the day when the state denies us the right to resort to force ... ."

Supreme Court Justice Louis Brandeis, The Brandeis Guide to the Modern World, p. 212 (Alfred Lief editor, 1941).

Legal Use of Force

ALL ADVICE IN THIS CHAPTER should be researched by the reader and/ or you should seek an attorney for legal counsel.

In the United States of America, each state holds its own definition of when deadly force is justified, however they all follow similar language as, for instance, the Revised Code of Washington State:

RCW 9A.16.050

Homicide—By other person—When justifiable.

Homicide is also justifiable when committed either:

(1) In the lawful defense of the slayer, or his or

her husband, wife, parent, child, brother, or sister, or of any other person in his or her presence or company, when there is reasonable ground to apprehend a design on the part of the person slain to commit a felony or to do some great personal injury to the slayer or to any such person, and there is imminent danger of such design being accomplished; or

(2) In the actual resistance of an attempt to commit a felony upon the slayer, in his or her presence, or upon or in a dwelling, or other place of abode, in which he or she is.

> Any taking of a human life by another human is considered homicide.

As you try to wrap your brain around that use of legal jargon there is a simpler way to understand if you were within your legal right to defend your life using force, and that is through these three simple words: ability, opportunity and jeopardy.

Ability means an attacker had a weapon capable of causing death or serious bodily harm; whether it was a beer bottle, bat, or chair. If the weapon was being used to inflict a blow, your actions of self-defense were justified.

Opportunity means just as the word says. One must prove in a court of law that the attacker had the "opportunity"; they were in close distance to you for example, to use their "ability" against you.

Jeopardy can be equated to "intent". This is exemplified in two basic questions: Was the intent to carry out an attack? Was your life in jeopardy?

Massad Ayoob, an internationally recognized self-defense expert, put it best when justifying use of deadly force:

"Deadly force is justified only when undertaken to prevent imminent and otherwise unavoidable danger of death or grave bodily harm to the innocent."

If only life were that simple. Most cases of self-defense are complicated due to the different variables within them.

> The laws on deadly force vary from state to state. Take the time to learn the laws of your jurisdiction.

Instances of sexual abuse and rape can become life threatening to the victim, so take into account "ability", "opportunity" and "jeopardy", as well as Ayoob's words, and you should have a clear understanding if your actions of self-defense will be seen as justifiable in a court of law.

In the United Kingdom, to claim self-defense in a court of law one must prove you were defending against crimes committed by use of force.

According to the Crown Prosecution Service:

The basic principles of self-defence are set out in (Palmer v R, [1971] AC 814); approved in R v McInnes, 55 Cr App R 551:

"It is both good law and good sense that a man who is attacked may defend himself. It is both good law and good sense that he may do, but only do, what is reasonably necessary."

The common law approach as expressed in Palmer v R is also relevant to the application of section 3 Criminal Law Act 1967:

"A person may use such force as is reasonable in the circumstances in the prevention of crime, or in effecting or assisting in the lawful arrest of offenders or suspected offenders or of persons unlawfully at large."

> **Use only the level of force that is necessary to repel your attacker.**

Section 3 applies to the prevention of crime and effecting, or assisting in, the lawful arrest of offenders and suspected offenders. There is an obvious overlap between self-defence and section 3. However, section 3 only applies to crime and not to civil matters. So, for instance, it cannot afford a defence in repelling trespassers by force, unless the trespassers are involved in some form of criminal conduct.

The "reasonable use of force" is outlined as permissible if it is an act of:

"Self-defence, defence of another, defence of property, prevention of crime, and/or lawful arrest."

When prosecutors are reviewing the reasonableness of the use of force you employed in an attack, they consider two things which could be equated to the US's standard of "jeopardy":

> Was your use of force reasonable and was it necessary?

Was the use of force necessary in the circumstance?

Was the force used reasonable in the circumstance?

These standards allow a lot of wiggle room for a jury to prosecute a person who defended themselves because they saw their method of defense "unreasonable" for the circumstances.

Once again, taking into consideration Ayood's words would be helpful.

The action of self-defense which uses force is a very serious matter and one that will affect the rest of your life, not only from an emotional, mental and spiritual sense, but also from your business to relationships with your family and friends. We are not talking about a small matter here and the consequences could be great.

That being said, you must protect your life at all costs. This should be your number one priority.

My opinion is that the best fight to win is the one you never had. Avoiding situations where you might need to use physical force is easily done, however sometimes fate deals you a bad hand and you have to respond.

Trusting your instinct and how to handle a threat is the best reaction, but you should be trained in order to be able to asses at what level you need to respond to a threat.

> If you have to use deadly force, it will change your life forever.

Do I choke out this guy and get away to call for help?

He has a knife and I'm unarmed; what do I do?

The man is shooting a whole restaurant of innocent people. I've got my concealed gun; should I engage?

A lot of these questions are answered in the reflex of your training. You often don't have time to think things through, you just react. That is why the person with whom you train and what you learn is very important. You could be learning techniques that would potentially incriminate you, while all along you thought it was legal.

Again, it is never wrong to defend and preserve

your life or another's. That is always your top priority.

How you determine a fight has escalated to a life and death circumstance depends heavily on your training. I cannot reiterate this enough: GET THE RIGHT TRAINING.

Pick someone whose focus is self-defense and has nothing to do with competition – that means whether it is jujutsu, shooting or knife fighting. The rules of engagement are completely different and are considered a separate art. It says it in the name: "competition", "sport."

Also, when deciding with whom to train for handgun courses, choose someone who knows the law and what a citizen in day-to-day life needs to learn. Many trainers might teach you what cops or our military learn. Each of these people have different end goals and are held to a different standard of the law.

> Get as much high-quality training as you can. It can save your life.

As a civilian, you need to train at this level, so you don't pick up any habits that might incriminate you.

Helpful Resources

1. One of the best things you can do (as some-one who carries a gun for self defense) is to take a class taught by Massad Ayoob called *Judicious Use of Deadly Force*. The class is three days of intense classroom instruction on the nature of deadly force, when you are justified in using it, and what are the effects it will have on you. Massad Ayoob is widely considered to be the world's leading authority on use of deadly force. The class is called *MAG 20/Classroom – Armed Citizens' Rules of Engagement*: You can register for this class by going to the Massad Ayoob Group website at: www.massadayoobgroup.com.

2. If you can't take the above course, at least read the book by Massad Ayoob titled *In the Gravest Extreme.* It is available on Amazon.com or anywhere else books are sold.

Chapter 6

Women Who

"Train the Dog"

"[Disarmament] palsies the hand and brutalizes the mind: an habitual disuse of physical forces totally destroys the moral; and men lose at once the power of protecting themselves, and of discerning the cause of their oppression." Joel Barlow, Advice to the Privileged Orders in the Several States of Europe: Resulting From the Necessity and Propriety of a General Revolution in the Principle of Government, Part I, page 45 (1792).

Women Who "Train the Dog"

SPEAKING OF TRAINING, WOMEN in our society need to ask themselves why so many men think it is permissible to treat us with such disregard and blatant lack of self-control.

Well, like I said before, your training relies on how you react. If a man is used to women throwing themselves at him to gain one step on the career ladder, then it is expected he might proposition the next woman for sexual favors for job advancement.

His actions are horrendous and not every woman floats in that kind of boat; but the women who do set sail in that exchange should consider the other women they are jeopardizing.

The case is quite clear in Hollywood and Washington, D.C.

Dozens, if not hundreds, of women nationwide

have revealed the sexual abuses and rapes that were forced on them by the men in the "big offices" and the allegations have been staggering.

Unwanted touching and rape are the most common accusations.

Now, I understand a lot of women who were forced in this "exchange" for a career promotion didn't want these actions to happen. You are in no way at fault for what happened to you.

> Women who sleep with their bosses to get a promotion are not real feminists.

My attention is on those women who do it deliberately. You set a precedent for other women which they will not agree to, causing crimes like sexual assault and rape.

Ladies, if you want to get higher on the career ladder, do it by virtue of your work and self-worth. Be someone with integrity and honor, so that when you get promoted you know it is based on your merit and not because you slept with the boss.

Isn't that what being a feminist is all about?

Equal to men?

If career women who sleep with their bosses to get a promotion claim to be feminists... they are greatly mistaken. I highly doubt Emmeline Pankhurst, founder of the Suffragette movement, would approve of such behavior.

This mentality of being "equal to men" has diverged into an ugly new feminism. Equal opportunity for work, the right to vote, study, hunt, shoot, eat, breathe and achieve makes sense.

However, the new "free the nipple" feminism which has women marching down main street topless, or sometimes stark naked, completely degrades women. As if the only way we can get attention for a just cause is by flashing our tits.

Come on, ladies!

I bet some man like Harvey Weinstein came up with that form of protest.

> Marching down Main street naked doesn't teach men to respect you.

Today's feminists tell society the only way to solve the sexual abuse and rape epidemic is to "teach men not to rape." How do feminists expect to do that when they teach females to engage in behavior like this?

Marching down Main Street completely naked doesn't teach men to respect you. It only gives them more opportunity to see naked women without watching porn or going to a strip club.

This isn't equality, ladies. It's a free peep show.

If you want real respect from people, here are some tips: conduct yourself in a respectful and courteous manner; always do the right thing; tell the truth and be good to others.

This advice holds true for men and women.

Holy smokes!

Did I just solve the equality issue?

Hmmmm…

Women's suffrage

The right to vote for women was a long-fought process that spanned decades. On the following dates, these countries granted women the right to vote.

1. 1881, the Isle of Man (off the coast of Ireland)

2. 1893, the British colony of New Zealand

3. 1894, the colony of South Australia

4. 1913, Norway

5. 1915, Denmark

6. 1917, Canada

7. 1918, Britain and 30 other countries.

8. 1919, Austria and the Netherlands

9. 1920, The United States

Chapter 7

Don't Cry Rape if

it Didn't Happen

"As of oligarchy so of tyranny ... Both mistrust the people, and therefore deprive them of their arms."

Aristotle, *Politics*, Book 5, part x (Benjamin Jowett translator; originally written 350 b.c.)

Don't Cry Rape if it Didn't Happen

FINALLY, THE WOMEN WHO ARE worse offenders than the misguided feminists of today, are the ones who cry rape to intentionally harm someone when it didn't happen.

By all means, you are among the vilest beings out there.

The actions you take not only damage the life of the man or woman you falsely accuse, but also the very victims who have gone through such horrendous experiences.

For the alleged attacker, who did nothing to you, their whole life is negatively affected. From personal relationships, to their careers and finances, all are damaged from a false statement.

And in this day and age, it doesn't take much effort to do so, just a few social media posts and everyone is labeling the accused as a rapist or sexual abuser. Take for instance civil rights activist Tarana Burke's #MeToo movement.

> The #MeToo movement is all about survivors supporting survivors.

In her own words during an interview with Business Insider on December 13, 2017, in an article titled "Tarana Burke on why she created the #MeToo movement — and where it's headed," she stated:

"#MeToo is essentially about survivors supporting survivors. And it's really about community healing and community action. Although we can't define with [sic] healing looks like for people, we can we can [sic] set the stage and give people the resources to have access to healing. And that means legitimate things like policies and laws that change that support [sic] survivors."

That is all well and good, however women who have been using this "MeToo" hashtag (#) have been misguided as to what sexual assault and rape is; and wrongly accusing men of these crimes.

Off the back of this movement, Moria Donugan published a list in which women claimed to have revealed instances of such offenses. The majority of them had absolutely nothing to do with workplace harassment.

Andrew Sullivan writes in his article for the New York Magazine on January 12, 2018 titled "It's Time to Resist the Excesses of #MeToo."

"Someone is accused of "creepy DMs or texts especially when drunk," "weird lunch dates," or "being handsy — at the very least — with women at parties.

One man is accused of "secretly removing condom during sex," with no claim of workplace misconduct at all.

Another is damned for "flirting," another for taking "credit for ideas of women of color," another for "multiple employee affairs, inappropriate conversation, in general a huge disgusting sleaze ball.

> Women have been wrongly accusing men of rape and sexual assault.

And this chorus of minor offenses is on the same list as brutal rapes, physical assaults, brazen threats, unspeakable cruelty, violence, and misogyny. But hey, take it all with a grain of salt!"

The accusations will probably forever linger in the accused's professional and personal life; people constantly questioning whether they did or did not commit

> The #MeToo movement sometimes abuses the due process rights of men.

a serious offense.

Furthermore, such a list calls into question due process.

Actress Catherine Deneuve signed an open letter, along with 100 other French women, who bring up this rule of law:

"This expedited justice already has its victims, men prevented from practicing their profession as punishment, forced to resign, etc., while the only thing they did wrong was touching a knee, trying to steal a kiss, or speaking about "intimate" things at a work dinner, or sending messages with sexual connotations to a woman whose feelings were not mutual."

What these French ladies understand is that they don't live life as victims of men, completely helpless or powerless. Therefore they don't feel the need to yell "RAPE" when nothing actually happened, but rather enjoy interactions with men when it turns flirtatious:

"A woman can, in the same day, lead a professional team and enjoy being the sexual object of a man, without being a 'slut', nor a cheap accomplice of the patriarchy."

Feminism today has turned men into spineless pansies. A poll conducted by YouGov can prove it too.

According to the Economist's column on the poll titled "Over-friendly, or sexual harassment? It depends partly on whom you ask", published on Nov 17th, 2017, one can conclude the following:

More than one-third of millenials (18-30) believe that it is "always/usually" sexual harassment if a man who is not a woman's romantic partner compliments her looks.

Of these same millenials, 1 in 4 females believe it is "always/usually" sexual harassment if a male asks a female out for a drink.

With that kind of statistics floating around, it is a wonder any man would approach another woman ever again; and, ladies, the next time you're out and no guy comes up to you or flirts with you, we have ourselves to blame.

> According to millenials, asking a woman out for a drink is sexual harassment.

As outlined in Chapter 2, according to the U.S. Equal Employment Opportunity Commission, sexual harassment is defined as:

"It is unlawful to harass a person (an applicant or employee) because of that person's sex. Harassment can include "sexual harassment" or

unwelcome sexual advances, requests for sexual favors, and other verbal or physical harassment of a sexual nature.

"Harassment does not have to be of a sexual nature, however, and can include offensive remarks about a person's sex. For example, it is illegal to harass a woman by making offensive comments about women in general.

> Offensive remarks about a person's sex is a form of sexual harassment.

"Both victim and the harasser can be either a woman or a man, and the victim and harasser can be the same sex.

"Although the law doesn't prohibit simple teasing, offhand comments, or isolated incidents that are not very serious, harassment is illegal when it is so frequent or severe that it creates a hostile or offensive work environment or when it results in an adverse employment decision (such as the victim being fired or demoted).

The harasser can be the victim's supervisor, a supervisor in another area, a co-worker, or someone who is not an employee of the employer, such as a client or customer."

Asking someone out for a drink or complimenting their looks hardly is sexual harassment.

The #MeToo movement, rather than actually giving a voice to the real victims of sexual abuse and rape, has turned into a "witch hunt" against men. Something that should have never happened.

Scarlett Johansson hit the nail on the head during her speech at the Women's March in Los Angeles, 2018, where she said:

> The #MeToo movement has morphed into a witch hunt against men.

"I never completely absorbed the "Me Too" phrase because I took the phrase at face value. But I've come to realize that while Me Too means different things to different people, to me it is very simply the ability to empathize with the visceral realities of this condition. I want to move forward, and for me moving forward means my daughter growing up in a world where she doesn't have to be a victim of what has cruelly become the social norm. That she doesn't have to fit into the bindings of the female condition. Time's up on the female condition.

"Gender equality can't just exist outside ourselves, it must exist within. We must take responsibility, not just for our actions, but for ourselves. We must make it our responsibility to feed our own healthy ego, to teach our children to exercise their own autonomy and ego strength

by leading by example. I have recently introduced a new phrase in my life that I would like to share with you: "No more pandering". No more feeling guilty about hurting people's feelings when something doesn't feel right for me. I have made a promise to myself to be responsible for myself. That in order to trust my instincts I must first respect them."

> Gender equality includes taking responsibility for our own actions.

Johansson understands the #WarriorChick mentality: taking your life and its responsibility in your own hands and depending on no one to protect it.

So what is next for the feminist movement?

First off, ditch the witch hunt on men and rather push for a culture where males respect females because the ladies deserve it, and sex isn't pursued as if it was some casual, emotionless action.

Secondly, ladies, have the confidence from within – and backed up by your knowledge of self-defense – to know what you want when interacting with a man.

However, to label a man's awkward, gross and/or entitled sexual advances towards you as "criminal" is quite absurd and only shows how insecure you are with yourself. So, don't do that. Get real empowerment instead.

Should the feminist movement choose to continue down this current "#MeToo" path, women who have actually gone through the assault others have only claimed to have experienced, will be forced to prove a crime to a suspicious justice system due to said "feminists."

Something which I believe no one actually wants: for the real victims of such horrendous crimes to be voiceless and unheard.

Our justice system must crack down on people who falsely accuse others of rape or sexual assault with the intent of purposely damaging that person's reputation. They should receive severe punishment, including a hefty fine and a long-term jail sentence.

> In the long run, these false accusations against men are a disservice to real victims of sexual harassment.

This type of behavior should quickly dissolve, if the above consequences are enforced, because perpetrators will see no immediate value in the action anymore.

One such case is Jemma Beale, a 25-year-old woman from west London. She made allegations of being seriously sexually assaulted by six different men, and raped by nine others. All the men were strangers and Beale claimed the instances happened four different times over the course of three years.

In July of 2017, the 25-year-old was found guilty at the Southwark crown court of four counts of perjury and four counts of perverting the course of justice, and sentenced to ten years in jail.

The Guardian published an article on August 24, 2017, titled "Woman jailed for 10 years for making series of false rape claims," which outlined the details of the case; including a very poignant statement from the judge:

> **Jemma Beale was jailed for 10 years for making a series of false rape claims.**

Sentencing her on Thursday, the judge, Nicholas Loraine-Smith, said: "This trial has revealed, what was then not obvious, that you are a very, very convincing liar and you enjoy being seen as a victim.

"The prosecution described your life as a 'construct of bogus victimhood'."

Madeleine Wolfe, prosecuting, told the court police spent 6,400 hours investigating Beale's claims at a cost of at least £250,000, and the trial cost at least £109,000.

Lawrence Henderson, defending, said Beale maintains her innocence and was considering an appeal against the sentence.

He told the court: "Ms Beale stands by the claims she made in this matter and if she had her time again she would again plead not guilty to these matters and contest the trial."

Beale from Bedfont, west London, sat with her arms crossed as she was jailed for a total of 10 years, with the judge branding her behaviour as "manipulative".

He said: "These offences usually began as a drunken attempt to get your partner's sympathy or perhaps to arouse her jealousy.

"They each began impulsively, but what is particularly chilling is the manner in which you persisted in making allegations which you knew were untrue even to the extent of committing and repeating perjury."

He continued: "These false allegations of rape, false allegations which will inevitably be widely publicized, are likely to have the perverse impact of increasing the likelihood of guilty men going free.

The judge said she was a very convincing liar and enjoys being seen as a victim.

"Cases such as this bring a real risk that a woman who has been raped or sexually assaulted may not complain to the police for fear of not being

believed."

Judge Nicholas Loraine-Smith's ruling should be held as a precedent in cases of false claims of "sexual harassment/assault, and/or rape."

Ladies, it is time we change this "construct of bogus victimhood" and turn into a #WarriorChick.

Chapter 8

What Defines a

#WarriorChick?

"A really strong woman
accepts the war she went
through and is ennobled
by her scars,"

Carly Simon.

What Defines a #WarriorChick?

THIS BOOK GIVES ALL THE TOOLS you need to turn from a #MeToo victim, into a #WarriorChick; but to spell it out for you, someone who is a #WarriorChick:

1. has the confidence to fight injustices committed against herself in the moment,

2. is secure in her own skin;

3. knows how to defend and protect her life and the lives of her loved ones;

4. is able to think for herself;

5. doesn't volunteer herself to be put in vulnerable situations;

6. can live her life ready to take on the challenges each day brings, and do it smiling;

7. refuses to ever be defined as a victim.

Take to heart the advice given in this book and, hopefully, we can change the future of men's and women's interactions for the better, one in which no person feels threatened and mutual respect and consideration are given to every individual.

Regis with her childhood friend
Delphine exploring the park.

Regis' first warthog, which was hunted in South Africa with her 9.3x74 double rifle using open sights.

(From left to right) Glenn Kendall, Regis Giles, and Doug Giles, having a quick breakfast before embarking on their morning safari.

(From left to right) Hannah Giles, Jex Fontaine, and Regis Giles at the Valente Brothers Jujutsu winter belt ceremony of 2015, where Hannah was promoted to her black belt.

ABOUT THE AUTHOR: In 2001, at nine years of age, Regis Giles began training at Valente Brothers Jujutsu Academy in Miami, Florida, one of the premier self-defense schools in the world. She became their first female black belt in 2014.

Since 2007 Regis has helped women and children learn how to adequately defend themselves against a physical attack. She is quite adept at both group and private instruction.

Giles is an internet and media personality, creator of girlsjustwannahaveguns.com, and has been featured in: ELLE magazine, Variety, the Daily Mail, BBC, ABC, CNN, CBS Miami, & Fox News.

Regis' goal is to help people protect their lives by becoming proficient in self-defense, which, obviously, will lead to a drop in violent crimes, and promote healthier communities full of respect and dignity.

Learn about all things Regis Giles at her website

www.girlsjustwannahaveguns.com

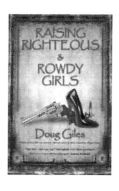

It has been said that daughters are God's revenge on fathers for the kind of men they were when they were young. Some would say that both Doug Giles and I, given our infamous pasts, are charter members of that club. However, Doug and I know that his two wonderful daughters and my equally wonderful daughter and two granddaughters are truly God's fantastic gift. With the wisdom of hindsight and experience Doug has written the ultimate manual for dads on raising righteous and rowdy daughters who will go out into the world well prepared- morally, physically, intellectually and with joyful hearts- to be indomitable and mighty lionesses in our cultural jungle. Through every raucous and no-holds-barred page, Doug, the incomparable Dad Drill Sergeant, puts mere men through the paces to join the ranks of the few, the proud, and the successful fathers of super daughters. The proof of Doug Giles' gold-plated credentials are Hannah and Regis Giles- two of the most fantastic, great hearted and accomplished young ladies I have ever known. This is THE BOOK that I will be giving the father of my two precious five and three year old granddaughters. Tiger Mom meet Lion Dad!

— Pat Caddell

Fox News Contributor —

73628389R00073

Made in the USA
San Bernardino, CA
07 April 2018